S0-DVE-147

December 2009

DISCARD

f
FE

★ ★

DELAWARE

by Jonatha A. Brown

GARETH STEVENS
GS
PUBLISHING
A Member of the WRC Media Family of Companies

Please visit our web site at: www.garethstevens.com
For a free color catalog describing Gareth Stevens Publishing's
list of high-quality books and multimedia programs, call
1-800-542-2595 (USA) or 1-800-387-3178 (Canada).
Gareth Stevens Publishing's fax: (877) 542-2596.

Library of Congress Cataloging-in-Publication Data

Brown, Jonatha A.
    Delaware / Jonatha A. Brown.
        p. cm. — (Portraits of the states)
    Includes bibliographical references and index.
    ISBN-10: 0-8368-4698-2 — ISBN-13: 978-0-8368-4698-0 (lib. bdg.)
    ISBN-10: 0-8368-4715-6 — ISBN-13: 978-0-8368-4715-4 (softcover)
    1. Delaware—Juvenile literature. I. Title. II. Series.
    F164.3.B763   2007
    971.5—dc22   2005036634

This edition first published in 2007 by
Gareth Stevens Publishing
A Weekly Reader Company
1 Reader's Digest Rd.
Pleasantville, NY 10570-7000 USA

This edition copyright © 2007 by Gareth Stevens, Inc.

Editorial direction: Mark J. Sachner
Project manager: Jonatha A. Brown
Editor: Catherine Gardner
Art direction and design: Tammy West
Picture research: Diane Laska-Swanke
Indexer: Walter Kronenberg
Production: Jessica Morris and Robert Kraus

Picture credits: Cover, © Paul Rezendes/www.paulrezendes.com; p. 4
© Jeff Greenberg/PhotoEdit; p. 5 © Elinor Benes/Visuals Unlimited; pp. 6, 11
© North Wind Picture Archives; p. 8 © MPI/Getty Images; p. 12 © CORBIS; pp.
15, 16, 18, 22, 28 © Mike Biggs, www.mikebiggsphotography.com; pp. 21, 26 ©
Pat & Chuck Blackley; p. 24 © Gibson Stock Photography; p. 25 © AP Images;
p. 27 © James P. Rowan; p. 29 Courtesy of Harrington Raceway

Printed in the United States of America

2 3 4 5 6 7 8 9 10 09 08 07

CONTENTS

Words that are defined in the Glossary appear
in **bold** the first time they are used in the text.

On the Cover: The harbor at Lewes is home to all kinds of boats. This
pretty harbor is on the Lewes-Rehoboth Canal in southern Delaware.

Introduction

If you could visit Delaware, where would you go? Would you head for a sandy ocean beach? Would you visit Lewes, where you can see the remains of a ship that sank long ago? Perhaps you would go to Newark. There you could watch figure skaters practice at a famous training rink.

All of these things and more await you in Delaware. Millions of visitors come to this state every year. They enjoy bustling cities and lovely old towns. They relax at sandy beaches and quiet state parks. Delaware is a small state with a great deal to offer!

A beautiful day begins at the Indian River Inlet.

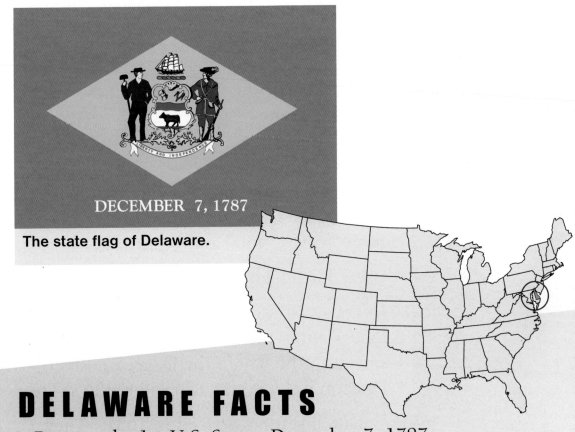

DECEMBER 7, 1787

The state flag of Delaware.

DELAWARE FACTS

- Became the 1st U.S. State: December 7, 1787
- Population (2006): 853,476
- Capital: Dover
- Biggest Cities: Wilmington, Dover, Newark, Milford
- Size: 1,954 square miles (5,061 square kilometers)
- Nickname: The First State
- State Tree: American holly
- State Flower: Peach blossom
- State Insect: Ladybug
- State Bird: Blue hen chicken

History

The first people to live in Delaware were Native Americans. They arrived about six hundred years ago. The Lenni Lenape and Nanticoke tribes hunted and fished. In the summers, they grew corn, beans, and squash. They also ate wild roots, leaves, nuts, and berries.

Early Europeans

In 1609, a Dutch ship sailed into Delaware Bay. Henry Hudson was on the ship. He sailed up the bay to the Delaware River. Hudson did not stay to explore the shore.

Dutch settlers arrived in 1631. They landed near what is now Lewes and tried to start a town. Their settlement did not last long. They argued with a Native chief and were killed by his men.

In the 1600s, Swedish ships brought many settlers to Delaware.

Seven years later, a group of Swedes arrived. They built Fort Christina near what is now the city of Wilmington. It became the first long-lasting white settlement in Delaware.

Soon, people from Finland joined the Swedes. They built the first log houses in North America.

Delaware Bay offered a harbor for ships. The Delaware River also was important. It provided a route inland from the sea. These two bodies of water made the Delaware area important to countries that relied on trade and shipping. At this time, the Dutch had the biggest shipping **empire** in the world. They did not

FUN FACTS

What's in a Name?

In 1610, a British sea captain reached Delaware by mistake. He was sailing for Baron De La Warr, the governor of the Virginia colony. A storm blew his ship off course, and he ended up in Delaware Bay. He named the bay for the governor. Many years later, the state took its name from the bay.

IN DELAWARE'S HISTORY

What Happened to the Natives?

When white settlers came to this land, the Natives suffered. White people had diseases that made the Lenni Lenape very sick. Many died. Those who survived were forced to move west. By 1732, most of the Lenni Lenape had left Delaware.

want anyone else to control the bay and the river. So the Dutch built their own fort and fought with the Swedes and Finns.

The Dutch took control of the area in 1655. They began to bring Africans here to work as slaves. Most slaves worked in tobacco fields and in settlers' homes.

A British Colony

The British also wanted this land. They struggled with the Dutch for control. First one country and then the other took over. Finally, in 1674, Britain won.

The British founded the Pennsylvania **Colony** in 1682. Delaware was part of this colony. More white settlers came here to live. Some helped build ships. Others grew tobacco, corn, and wheat. Slaves still did most of the work on some Delaware farms.

The three counties in the south did not seem like a part of Pennsylvania. The people who lived in this area wanted to form their own colony. In 1704, they were allowed to set up their own assembly. Now, they could make their own laws. In 1775, the borders of the new colony were drawn.

At about this time, the people of Delaware passed a law against slavery. Slave owners could keep the slaves they had, but they could not bring more slaves here.

William Penn of Britain meets with the Lenni Lenape in 1682. They agree that their people should live in peace.

By the early 1770s, many colonists on the East Coast had tired of British rule. They wanted to be free. The Revolutionary War began in 1775 and lasted eight years. Thousands of colonists from Delaware joined the fight. They helped win the war.

The First State

In 1787, Delaware became the first state to accept the U.S. Constitution. This made it the first U.S. state. Before long, factories were built in Wilmington and other cities. They made gunpowder, flour, and cloth. The new state soon became a center for industry.

Slavery and the Civil War

In Southern states, many white people owned slaves. In most Northern states, slavery was against the law.

FUN FACTS

Breaking the Tie

Caesar Rodney was a colonial leader from Delaware. He was sick when the time came to vote on the Declaration of Independence in 1776. He stayed in bed and did not vote. Without him, the vote ended in a tie. Rodney soon learned of this result. So he got out of bed and rode his horse 80 miles (129 km) in the rain. He arrived at the meeting and broke the tie. Caesar Rodney cast his vote for freedom.

People in the two parts of the country did not agree. In 1860, the Southern states began leaving the **Union**. They formed their own country. They called it the Confederate States of America.

9

FACTS

Shortcut

In the 1820s, workers dug a canal across the state. The Chesapeake and Delaware Canal was 14 miles (23 km) long. The canal joined the Chesapeake Bay to the Delaware River. Ships could go straight from Baltimore, Maryland, to Delaware. The canal made this trip almost 300 miles (483 km) shorter!

The people in the North did not want the South to break away. The two sides started fighting the Civil War in 1861.

Some people in Delaware still owned slaves. Even so, the state stayed in the Union and fought for the North. After four years of fighting, the North won. Slavery was outlawed all over the nation.

Famous People of Delaware

"Judy" Johnson

Born: October 26, 1889, Snow Hill, Maryland

Died: June 15, 1989, Wilmington, Delaware

William Julius Johnson was a great baseball player. He became one of the best third basemen ever. Yet, Johnson could not play in the major leagues because he was black. He had to play in the **Negro** Leagues. Many years after he retired, the major leagues changed their rules. They let black players join their teams. Two teams hired Johnson to find black players for them. With his help, many African Americans began playing in the major leagues. Before Johnson died, he was made a member of the National Baseball Hall of Fame.

By 1880, New Castle had many small factories. It was also a center for shipping.

The 1900s

After the Civil War, Delaware kept growing. More factories were built, and the cities grew. By 1920, more people lived in cities than in the country.

The United States fought in two world wars in the first half of the 1900s. These wars were fought overseas. Many soldiers from Delaware fought. Other people stayed home to grow food, build ships,

Shipbuilding has always been big business in Delaware. This photo shows workers laying the hull of a steamship in 1892.

IN DELAWARE'S HISTORY

Black and White

Not everyone in Delaware did well in the 1900s. White people refused to hire African Americans for some jobs. They would not sell houses in all-white areas to black people, either. Many black people grew angry. They wanted good jobs and nice homes. Race riots broke out in Wilmington in the late 1960s. After the riots, new laws were passed. Now, no one can be kept from buying a home or being hired for a job because of skin color.

and make war supplies. By the mid-1940s, Dravo Shipyards in Wilmington was the biggest **employer** in the state. Eleven thousand people worked there.

Delaware Today

Today, Delaware is a rich state. It has good schools and healthy businesses. In 2000, the people of Delaware elected Ruth Ann Minner to be the governor. She was the state's first female governor.

1609	Henry Hudson sails into Delaware Bay
1638	Swedes found Fort Christina, the first long-lasting settlement in Delaware.
1674	The British gain control of Delaware.
1682	The British found the Pennsylvania Colony; the colony includes Delaware.
1704	The three counties of Delaware set up their own assembly to make laws.
1775	Delaware's borders are drawn.
1775–1783	Colonists in Delaware help fight the British in the Revolutionary War.
1787	Delaware becomes the first U.S. state.
1829	The Chesapeake and Delaware Canal opens.
1861–1865	Delaware fights on the side of the North during the Civil War.
1917–1918	Delaware helps the United States fight World War I.
1937	Nylon is created at the DuPont Corporation.
1941–1945	Delaware helps the United States fight World War II.
2000	Voters in Delaware elect Ruth Ann Minner as the state's first female governor.

People

Delaware is a small state. Yet, more people live here than in some of the larger states. More than 830,000 people live here. About three-fourths of them live in or near cities. Wilmington is the largest city in the state. It is in the far northern part of Delaware. This area is becoming crowded.

The southern part of the state has fewer cities. It has more farms and small towns. People live farther apart here than they do in the far north.

Hispanics

This chart shows the different racial backgrounds of people in Delaware. In the 2000 U.S. Census, 4.8 percent of the people in Alaska called themselves Latino or Hispanic. Most of them or their relatives came from places where Spanish is spoken. Hispanics do not appear on this chart because they may come from any racial background.

The People of Delaware

Total Population 853,476

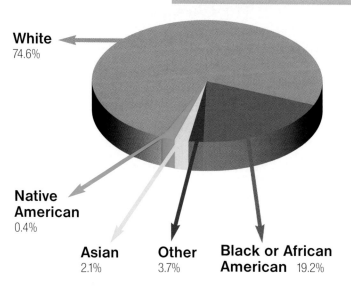

White
74.6%

Native
American
0.4%

Asian
2.1%

Other
3.7%

Black or African
American 19.2%

Percentages are based on the 2000 Census.

A Mix of People

More than 72,000 people live in Wilmington. The city is also a big center for banking.

About three out of four people who live in the state are white. Some of these white people can trace their families back to the Dutch, Swedes, and Finns who settled the area long ago. Others have ties to Britain, France, and Germany.

Only about 7 percent of the people who live here today were born in other countries. Many of these **immigrants** have come from Mexico and Asia.

More than 72,000 people live in Wilmington. The city is also a big center for banking.

Few people are moving here from Europe now.

Almost 20 percent of the people are African American. Many African Americans live in Wilmington. In fact, about one-half of the people in this city are black.

The Native **population** is small. Only a few thousand Natives still live here. Many of them are members of the Nanticoke tribe.

The University of Delaware is the largest and oldest university in the state. It is also a center for art, African American history and culture, and more.

Religion

As in the rest of the country, most of the people who live in this state are Christians. Methodists and Catholics make up the two largest Christian groups. A few hundred Amish live near Dover. They are Christians who live simply. The Amish do not use cars or electric lights. Delaware is home to Jews and people of other faiths, too.

Education

The state's first public school system was set up in 1829. These schools served only white children. After the Civil War ended, public schools for black children were set up. These schools were separate from white schools. Delaware's schools were **segregated**.

In 1954, the U.S. Supreme Court said segregation in schools was unfair. The Court ordered the school system to change. Even so, most schools in Delaware did not start to become racially mixed until the late 1970s. Now, public schools are open to all.

Newark is home to the first and oldest university in the state. This is the University of Delaware. It was founded in 1743. Today, this university serves about 18,000 students. The state has other universities and colleges, but the University of Delaware is the largest.

Famous People of Delaware

Thomas Garrett

Born: August 21, 1789, Upper Darby, Pennsylvania

Died: January 25, 1871, Wilmington, Delaware

Thomas Garrett was a Quaker who lived in Wilmington for many years. Quakers are Christians. They do not believe in fighting or keeping slaves. Garrett helped many slaves escape to freedom. The law forbade anyone to help a slave escape, but Garrett believed the law was wrong. In the mid-1800s, he became a "conductor" on the Underground Railroad. He helped more than twenty-seven hundred slaves reach the North. At one point, he was found guilty of helping a slave escape. Garrett had to pay a big fine, and he lost everything he owned. Even so, he kept helping slaves run away to freedom.

The Land

Delaware is one of the two smallest U.S. states. It is about 96 miles (154 km) long. The widest part of the state is 36 miles (58 km) across. It is shaped like a tall, thin triangle.

The land here is mostly low and flat. In fact, Delaware is the lowest state in the nation. Its hills are small, and its slopes are gentle.

The Piedmont Plateau

The state has two natural regions. They are the Piedmont **Plateau** and the Atlantic Coastal Plain.

The Piedmont Plateau lies in the far northern part of the state. A plateau is a large area that is higher than the land around it.

The Piedmont Plateau is a land of farms, forests, and rolling hills.

DELAWARE

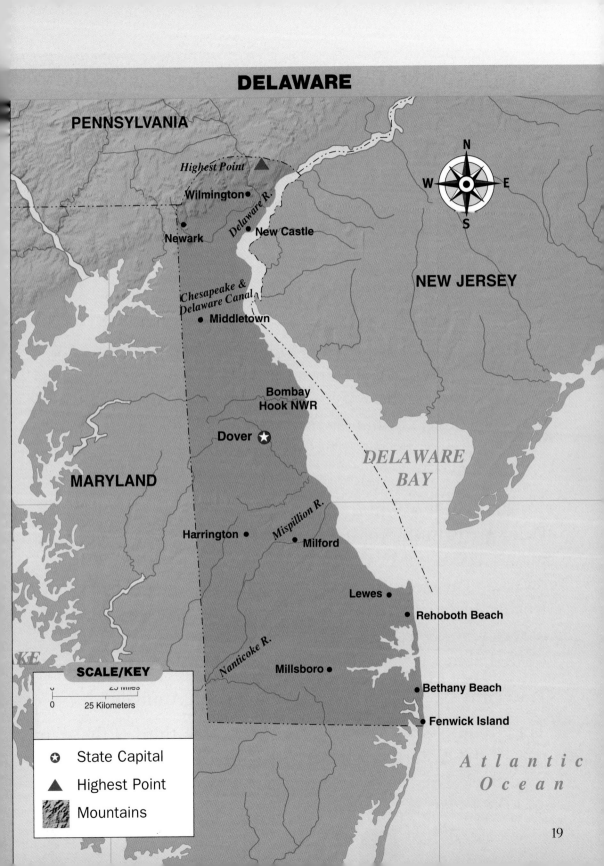

PENNSYLVANIA

Highest Point ▲

Wilmington ●

Delaware R.

Newark ●

● New Castle

*Chesapeake &
Delaware Canal*

● Middletown

NEW JERSEY

Bombay
Hook NWR

Dover ⊗

DELAWARE
BAY

MARYLAND

Mispillion R.

Harrington ●

● Milford

Lewes ●

● Rehoboth Beach

Nanticoke R.

Millsboro ●

● Bethany Beach

● Fenwick Island

Atlantic
Ocean

KE

SCALE/KEY

0   25 Miles

0   25 Kilometers

⊗   State Capital

▲   Highest Point

   Mountains

The highest point in Delaware is found in the plateau. It is Ebright Road in the northern part of the state. It is 448 feet (137 meters) above sea level.

The Atlantic Coastal Plain

The rest of the state is in the Atlantic Coastal Plain. The land is very low. Most of it is only about 60 feet (18 m) above sea level. Some of the land is covered by the ocean at high tide.

The richest soil in Delaware is in the coastal plain. The Great **Cypress** Swamp is also found here. It is farther north than any other cypress swamp in the United States.

Waterways

The Atlantic Ocean forms part of the eastern border of this state. The Delaware Bay and the Delaware River form

Major Rivers

Delaware River
280 miles (451 km) long

Nanticoke River
63 miles (101 km) long

Mispillion River
20 miles (32 km) long

the rest of this border. The Delaware River is the longest river in the state. It has long been used as a shipping route. Most other rivers in Delaware are too shallow for big boats.

Delaware has no big lakes. It does have many small lakes and ponds, however. The state's largest lakes were created by dams that were built on rivers and streams.

Plants and Animals

Almost one-third of the state is wooded. Pines, beeches, maples, and other trees grow here. Near the bay and the ocean, salt marshes cover large areas. **Cordgrass** and cattails grow on these wet stretches of land.

The white-tailed deer is the only big animal found in the state. Smaller animals include raccoons, foxes, and muskrats. These animals are common in most parts of Delaware. Mink, otter, and beaver are also found here.

This state is a great place for bird watching. Many kinds of birds fly through the area in the spring and fall. Some ducks, egrets, and herons live here all year long. Quail, doves, and pheasants are some of the common game birds.

FACTS

A Ragged Coast

This small state has only 28 miles (45 km) of ocean coastline. The shore along the ocean is very ragged. Including all of the bays, coves, and small inlets, the shoreline is 381 miles (613 km) long!

The salt marshes are home to mussels, many kinds of crabs, and other shellfish. Sea bass, bluefish, and other saltwater fish are found off the coast. Bass, catfish, and other freshwater fish swim in the rivers.

Spring and fall are the best times to see lots of birds at the Bombay Hook National Wildlife Refuge.

Economy

In its earliest days, Delaware was a farming state. The early settlers grew tobacco, wheat, and corn. They also grew peaches. In fact, peaches were so important that the peach blossom was named the state flower. Much later, disease killed the peach trees, so farmers began growing apples and other fruits.

Today, farming is less important than it once was. Most of Delaware's farms are in the central and southern parts of the state. Broiler chickens are the main farm product. Soybeans and corn are the top crops. Most of the soybean and corn harvest is used for chicken feed.

The Port of Wilmington is a busy place. Here, tourists enjoy a sail on a tall ship while a big cargo ship rests at anchor.

Factories and More

Long ago, factories helped this small state grow strong. Shipbuilding was the first big industry. A new kind of flour mill was invented here in 1785. Gunpowder was also an important product. Later, nylon was invented by the DuPont Corporation. Nylon was used in stockings and in the war supplies used during World War II. Today, chemicals are the state's leading product.

Shipping has long been a key industry. Now, banking is very important. **Tourism** is big business, too. Tourists sleep in hotels and eat at restaurants. They bring money into Delaware.

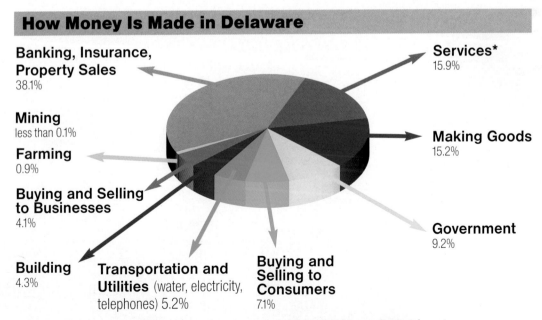

How Money Is Made in Delaware

Banking, Insurance, Property Sales
38.1%

Mining
less than 0.1%

Farming
0.9%

Buying and Selling to Businesses
4.1%

Building
4.3%

Transportation and Utilities (water, electricity, telephones) 5.2%

Buying and Selling to Consumers
7.1%

Services*
15.9%

Making Goods
15.2%

Government
9.2%

* Services include jobs in hotels, restaurants, auto repair, medicine, teaching, and entertainment.

Government

Dover is the capital of Delaware. The leaders of the state work in this city. The state government has three parts. They are the executive, legislative, and judicial branches.

Executive Branch

The job of this branch is to carry out the state's laws. The governor is the head of this branch. The lieutenant governor helps the governor lead the state. A group of people known as the cabinet also helps.

The Legislative Hall is in Dover. The members of the General Assembly meet here to make laws for the state.

Ruth Ann Minner was elected governor in 2000 and was reelected four years later. She was the first woman to serve as governor of Delaware.

Legislative Branch

The legislative branch is called the General Assembly. It has two parts. They are the Senate and the House of Representatives. The two groups work together to make state laws.

Judicial Branch

Judges and courts make up the judicial branch. They may decide whether people who have been **accused of** committing crimes are guilty.

Local Governments

Delaware has three counties. Each one is run by a team of people. Most towns and cities are led by a council and a mayor or city manager.

DELAWARE'S STATE GOVERNMENT

Executive		Legislative		Judicial	
Office	**Length of Term**	**Body**	**Length of Term**	**Court**	**Length of Term**
Governor	4 years	Senate (21 members)	4 years	Supreme (5 justices)	12 years
Lieutenant Governor	4 years	House of Representatives		Superior (19 judges)	12 years
		(41 members)	2 years	Court of Chancery (5 judges)	12 years

Things to See and Do

The Zwaanendael Museum shows what life was like for the early Dutch settlers.

If you like history, you are sure to enjoy Delaware. You might want to start at the Zwaanendael Museum in Lewes. From the outside, the building looks like a fancy Dutch town hall. Inside, displays tell exciting tales about the past. Some of the best exhibits come from a ship that sank in 1798. The ship and its contents lay on the ocean floor for nearly two hundred years. Now, items from the sunken ship help us learn about life long ago.

Wilmington is home to the Kalmar Nyckel Shipyard. The shipyard's displays show how shipbuilding helped this area grow. You can also see a tall ship at this museum. It looks just like the one that brought the first Swedish settlers to Delaware long ago.

For modern history, visit Dover Air Force Base. It is the largest Air Force base on the East Coast. A museum on the base traces the history of U.S. fighter planes.

Hit the Beach!

If you visit Delaware, be sure to leave time for a trip to the beach. Rehoboth Beach is a very popular choice. It has

These stone buildings were once used to make gunpowder. Today, you can visit this gunpowder mill at the Hagley Museum in Wilmington.

beautiful old mansions, ocean waves, and soft sand. Other favorite spots near the ocean are Bethany Beach and Fenwick Island. All of these beaches are in the southern part of the state.

In Delaware, not all of the fun takes place at the beach. You can ride horses on about 150 miles (241 km) of trails in state parks. State parks are also great places to hike, ride bikes, and go camping. The Bombay Hook National Wildlife Refuge is not far from Dover. It is one of

Famous People of Delaware

Annie Jump Cannon

Born: December 11, 1863, Dover, Delaware

Died: April 13, 1941, Cambridge, Massachusetts

When Annie Jump Cannon was a child, she loved looking at the nighttime sky. Her mother taught her the names of many stars. When she was older, Cannon went to college. She studied stars and became an **astronomer**. She discovered many stars that no one had seen before. Today, Cannon is remembered as one of the first great female astronomers.

Rehoboth Bay offers all kinds of fun on a hot summer day! These people are wind surfing on the bay. Other people may be sunning on the beach and playing in the waves.

Harness racing is an exciting sport. Many people come to Harrington Raceway to watch the horses and their drivers. This track is quite famous.

the best spots in the region to see many kinds of birds.

Sports

Wilmington has a minor league baseball team, but the state is best known for other sports. The University of Delaware has an excellent figure skating club. Tara Lipinski honed her skills there. She went on to win a gold medal at the 1998 Winter Olympics.

Harness racing has many fans in this state. One of the oldest tracks in the United States is in Harrington. Both Wilmington and Dover have well-known tracks, too.

Wilmington also hosts a major golf **tournament** for women each year. It takes place at the DuPont Country Club.

accused of — blamed for

astronomer — a scientist who studies the stars and planets

colony — a group of people living in a new land but controlled by the place they came from

cordgrass — a stiff grass that grows in salt marshes along the coast of an ocean

cypress — an evergreen tree that has small, tightly packed leaves that look like scales

empire — a very large business operation that is controlled by one group or person

employer — a person who hires people to do work

immigrants — people who leave one country to live in another country

mansion — a very large house

Negro — having to do with dark-skinned people who trace their families to Africa

peninsula — a body of land that juts out into a body of water

plateau — a large raised area of land with steep sides

population — the number of people who live in a place such as a state

segregated — separated by skin color

tourism — businesses that serve people who travel for fun

tournament — a sports competition

Union — the United States of America

Books

The Colony of Delaware. The Thirteen Colonies and the Lost Colony (series). Susan Whitehurst (Power Kids Press)

Delaware. Rookie Read-About Geography (series). Kelly Bennett (Children's Press)

The Delaware People. Native Peoples (series). Allison Lassieur (Bridgestone Books)

F Is for First State: A Delaware Alphabet. Discover America State by State (series). Carol Crane (Sleeping Bear Press)

Horseshoe Crabs and Shorebirds: The Story of a Food Web. Victoria Crenson (Marshall Cavendish)

The Underground Railroad. Raymond Bial (Houghton Mifflin)

Web Sites

Visit Delaware
www.visitdelaware.com

Delaware Kids' Page
www.state.de.us/gic/kidspage/

Delaware (Lenape) Tribe of Indians
www.delawaretribeofindians.nsn.us/

Enchanted Learning: Delaware
www.enchantedlearning.com/usa/states/delaware/

INDEX